Twentieth Century *Revisited*

for my shepherds and guides

for my parents and sister

for my husband, family and friends.

Una O'Higgins O'Malley

TWENTIETH CENTURY REVISITED

with an appreciation by Conor Brady

ARLEN
HOUSE

First published by Arlen House in August 2003:

Arlen House
PO Box 222
Galway
Ireland

email: arlenhouse@ireland.com

ISBN 1–903631–43–2 paperback

Printed by: ColourBooks, Baldoyle, Dublin 13

contents

Twentieth Century *Revisited*

ACKNOWLEDGEMENTS

Some of these poems have appeared in *Poetry Ireland Review; Tain - the Australian-Irish Network; Jumping the Bus Queue* edited by Mary Rose Callaghan; *The Backyards of Heaven* edited by John Ennis and Stephanie McKenzie; the *O'Malley journal;* and in the author's memoirs *From Pardon and Protest* (Arlen House, 2001).

My special thanks are due to Dorothy Carpenter, Susan Byrne, Pat Schneider and Gerard Quinn, as well as to those who took part with me in the groups which they led. I am also indebted to Jonathan Williams, Padraig J. Daly, Joan McBreen and Mary Rose Callaghan for their encouragement, and to many other friends.

The photography of Roy Hewson on the jacket of the book is much appreciated, as is the kindness of Elena von Munchow of the National Gallery in facilitating his work on the portrait of my mother.

I deeply appreciate the supportive words of Conor Brady.

My publisher Alan Hayes seems to have paid special attention to the Inaugural Address of our President when she invited us to 'Come to the Edge'. May he be rewarded for his courage.

Ambition

for Padraig J. Daly in gratitude

It's not that I aspire to be an epic poet
or the last of the great romantics
I just want to search
beneath the to and fro' of things
and feel the pulse of the heartbeat
hidden there, then find a language
that would show (not tell)
its secret meaning.

I would write something
that my friends could keep
as they do their photographs
something that would speak
of love and honesty and humour
and that might help repay
the expenses of my privileged journey.

A Widow's Child

She kept a powder-puff of pale pink swansdown
placed in a bowl of coral-coloured glass
centred on her table;
candlesticks on either side,
made of the same pink crystal,
framed her pale face as she gazed
intently in her mirror.
Between them stood a cut-glass perfume-spray
with rubber bulb secured in silken netting
and a little dish of matching coloured glass
with upstretched finger to receive her rings.
Her sister made a frilly petticoat
to wrap around this marble table
hiding its naked timber uprights.
An ottoman stretched before the sun-filled window
covered in cheerful cretonne
and when it was cold, the gas-fire hissed a friendly
singsong,
glowing in shades of pink and green and azure.

Within that room was focused all my being;
to it I turned for warmth, for comfort and for loving.
It took some time to understand the carved mahogany bed
was far too large for her small figure
and why the mirrored wardrobe, which was made for two,
held only female garments.
Three brass jugs that once warmed shaving-water
stood empty on the cupboard.
It took some time to realise
my mother too might need some comforting.

Pro Patria Mori

(reflections on the Michael Collins film and the biography of Hazel Lady Lavery)

It is no doubt appropriate
that each should make their own of him
since he has fallen.
Self-justified assassins celebrate,
proud colleagues elevate his name
on lofty cenotaphs.
His weeping widow tries
to comfort his small children,
his lover may decide
to save her story for a later day.
Biographers, historians, all have their say;
poets, painters, sculptors
must quickly add him to portfolios.
Grandsons will struggle to recall his dates
for school examinations
and an Oscar-bearing actor may reach for the stars
on his broad shoulders!

Meanwhile, contrastingly, his generous bones
in patient, uncomplaining silence lie:
'Dulce et decorum est pro patria mori'.

INSPIRATION

I mosey in my little mouse-brown car
down fog-bound avenues of my mind
seeking my errant muse
now totally 'as láthair'.

And if I should find her
I shall bring her home
and make her cups of tea
and sit her down at my computer
(for I have work I cannot do without her).

I'll borrow her ideas and call them mine
and save them in 'my files'
never pretending they are just on loan
from a mysterious other.

RESTORATION

So – is it all unravelling,
the ritual of book and candle,
of jewelled mitres and the golden staffs
of stern authority,
the labyrinths of polished corridors,
the swelling organs and the potted palms,
the whispered confidences
and the solemn portraits
done in oils to emphasise the ego?

Are we dealing with re-vision
in this new century?
The antique titles and the purple rings,
the convent parlours and the Confirmation banquets,
even the customary deferences – all are going,
disappearing back through time and time
from gold to brass to copper
and finally to carpenters' timber;
to the smooth carved wood of a shepherd's crook
and the cot of a simple manger,
to the savage strength of a criminal's cross
suspending in shame
our one necessity.

Are we tracing back and back to bread and wine
laid on a supper table,
to the problems of hungry lambs and sheep,
to the challenge of loving,
to an empty tomb laid bare
of the risen Saviour
and when we have got that far
will we then address His simple question
'Do you love me?'

In a Garden

for Andrew

So what is waste?
Agony beneath a plum
or olive tree?

Who put it in our hearts to understand
and further to agree
that the most loving Father
knows when to spread his arms
and welcome Home his children?

PRISONERS

(at the launch of Marie O'Neill life of Grace Plunkett)

Steeped in the memory of old Kilmainham
numbed by the cold within those rugged walls
we drink red wine and wish the book 'God Speed',
we, whom the legacy of Civil War had separated.
The tale of Joseph Plunkett's bride of just one day
Had brought us together where
some of the kindest words that I have heard
are spoken to me by a de Valera.

I go home wondering once more
whether the generations of partition
had really been essential? Was there no other way
we could have forged our present bond with Britain
and need a Dorothy Macardle or Nell Ryan
– my husband's aunt –
have gone on hunger-strike
while prisoners of my father?

Now it is past, or very nearly so,
except for those who still resist
the decommissioning of their grievances;
the rest of us are free at last
to drink the wine and smile into the eyes
of one another,
knowing all too well the price
that paid for it.

ON READING THE LETTERS OF MY FATHER TO HAZEL LAVERY

'Come take my hand' you say 'and walk upon the waters'.
'The waters of betrayal, Lord? Uncompassed and afraid,
bereft without my certainty, my Dunamase, my citadel,
bronze figure of antiquity in Churchill's ringing phrase?'

'But take my hand' you coax 'and tread upon the waters'.
'Deep waters of depression, dejection or despair?
Grey waters of bewilderment, of cynical surrender,
or shallows of distraction over which to sail elsewhere?'

'Come take my hand' you plead 'and test my shining
waters',
'come walk on sparkling waters in the radiance of the sun;
bright waters of complexity, humanity, diversity,
clear waters of forgiveness, of compassion and of love.

For absolutes belong to me and no-one else is sacred
And bronze can be the stuff of which false images are
formed;
And people are not images but flesh and blood and fragile,
Come, celebrate the doting 'hands-on' Father of them all!

Neighbourhood Watch

I caught a crescent moon at dawn
with single bridesmaid star
in sky of duck egg blue.
Behind the chimneys of the nearby houses
I saw the feathery plumes of pampas-grasses,
the wire around the tennis-courts
and goal-posts in the neighbouring school
in sabled silhouette.

But now both moon and star are gone,
the sky is blandly blue, washed out, unint'resting;
the creamy pampas waves but not majestically,
wild raucous shouts pervade the playing-fields
while wisps from chimneys tell of lives warmed up
in cheerful solidarity
(mostly the talk is bargains, bingo and the football).

Why do you call by with your silver moons
on opalescent back-drop?
Do you not know that we have tamed them all
or lost the key to codes which you are using?
Getting and spending, our exhausted powers
no longer comprehend your meaning.
Why haunt us with your signals?
Our undernourished souls
have powered off our mobiles.

ORPHANAGE

Somehow he struggled through his boyhood years
and later with grizzled curly hair
in tight-jawed Dublin voice
he would record his story to a poetry-class
in a distant University;
a straitened hunched-up piece
of only six or seven lines
it spoke of naked suffering
in a place that would forever
rhyme with pain.

Pentecost

Like a great wind rushing,
the Spirit swoops among the spruces,
pulses through the pine-trees,
waving, weaving, dancing,
churning, turning upside down
our preconceived ambitions,
laughing at our stuffiness,
sighing, weeping, moaning
at the trivialities
we count as treasures,
begging for attention
and the rearrangement
of priorities.
Remember, oh remember these,
the Spirit pleads;
the bread of faithfulness
the wine of fellowship,
water to wash your brother's aching feet.
Remember these, the Spirit pleads,
remember, oh remember these!

Sea

When we were young
the sea belonged to me,
to me and my sister,
the part of it, that is,
called Scotsman's Bay;
and I still look on it as mine.

Others may have a share in it, of course,
now that we seldom go there,
but nothing will ever take away
my sense of ownership,
not even the mighty ferries
now speeding through its waters.

There still remain our pools, our shrimps, our seaweed
and the great flat rock where we with friends produced
our entertainments.

Shalom

for Bill and Betty Ruder

On the sixtieth Dunkirk Day
we swirled through wind and rain
to Europe's most western Abbey
where we gathered with Jewish American friends
remembering the Kristalnacht, Treblinka, Birkenau,
and all that sea of grief that floods the soul
with those two words 'The Holocaust'.
Benedict, patron of Europe, had inspired the idea
affording forgiveness with his famous hospitality
so that we could take each others' hands
and confessing our shame, could pray the Kaddish
    together
as we wished to each 'Shalom'.

Then came the party;
the fun, the jokes, the laughter,
the songs, the 'party pieces'
the hopes for next year;
'See you in June!' they said 'we've already made our
bookings'.
As in their song beneath their faithful, very generous feet
the earth indeed did thunder 'We are here!'

- *Kylemore Abbey, 2000*

A SONG OF PRAISE

'Come, kiss and make friends'
the sunshine shyly said
after a week of absence
when thunder growled around the mountains
and lightning sparked and crackled in the radio;
'Come, kiss and be friends!
See how the birds are out about their business
not looking back or sulking
because of what has happened.
It is today, not yesterday
and I am going to paint the grass all golden;
don't think about the spikes of ice and snow
that linger in it
or worry if the road is frozen.
I'm working on it now
so you may safely drive to Mass
and offer your praise
to my Creator'.

Good Neighbours

Once upon a time
we lived across the road
from Camelot
where people of friendliness and fun
courtesy and charm
would make us welcome.
Our children revelled in nurseries
romped in its sheltered woodlands
danced in its vast ballroom
and enjoyed its lovely parties.
The hospitable house
seemed full of sunshine then
bright as the eyes of its young lord and lady
and the smiles of their willing helpers.
In those glad years we didn't realise
that darkness soon
would make its home with them
eating its stealthy, suffocating way
into the heart and soul
and very lifeblood too
of gracious, kindly, open,
undefended
Camelot

THE SNOWDROP

for Elizabeth, 27 May 2000

With flaxen hair curled high over slender neck
she bowed her head in welcome –
this was her first communion.
Later our satin-slippered girl
shed ivory organza gown
for nifty pedal-pushers
and frolicked with her family and friends
in joyful celebration.

Lament for a Mongrel Dog

'I loved your children utterly
and let them have their way with me
completely. I lightened dreary days for them
and frolicked in their games and taught them
how to fondle and be gentle.
I loved you, too, and did my best
to guard your home for you,
say, was it not enough?'

'Oh foolish pup!
you wandered from that home
and spying solemn sheep in distant field
thought it but sport to scatter and pursue them
all heedless they were heavy with their lambs
and now we have to answer with your life.
Oh friend – we loved you too
but love seems just a loser
this sad day'.

- *'White Lodge' 1970*

THE STORM (MID-JANUARY)

Today the lake was seriously angry
not just fretful, straining, threatening
but really furious – in humour with
the rolling thunder overhead
and the sudden sheets of lightning
that once again knocked out the electricity.
Now, having shown their strength
and overweening power,
the storm-clouds sweep away
to other unsuspecting townlands;
the fridge again ventures its bourgeois humming
and the boiler pulls itself together in the outhouse.
But the shelduck, imperturbable, experienced,
throughout the storm
has managed business as usual
just outside the harbour.

THRESHOLD

Those who once planted it have trod the path
of age, infirmity and death
and now the property is owned by absentees
who sometimes come and go –
depending on the fishing.

But though the neglected garden has gone wild
a soufflé, a pavlova, of palest pink-and-white
rhododendron
still celebrates the spring alone
beside the rusting silver railings
in beauty almost unbearable.

LIGHT

When God created light
did he first work in dark ruminative space
as is the way with other artists?

Did he rest among familiar shades before
dazzling, electrifying, shocking
his nascent world
into the reflection of his glory?

Remembering Toledo

Today perhaps I'll paint my toenails pink,
not heliotrope or red – though many like them so –
but terracotta pink like bricks in old Toledo;
and I will think of narrow winding streets
amid its ancient buildings. I will forget
the frenzied guide with bronzed and back-combed hair,
delivering a diatribe about its mysteries
to earnest oriental visitors, while overhead
the Coca-Cola signs mark out the way
towards McDonald's. I will just say
these feet have tiptoed over cobblestones of faith
and down long corridors of terracotta history.

THE VILLAGE

The river winds its drowsy way
under the old stone bridge
decked with valerian,
skirting the church built in the famine years
by hungry people,
bubbling dreamily behind the bright new restaurants
whose pinks and sometimes startling purples
ruffle the rich brown water
but never match the aching beauty
left behind in stained-glass windows
of the church where Clarke's cornelians,
his sapphires and his emeralds
are seldom noticed nowadays
except by the older tourists.
And the sea-green Connemara altar
no longer gleams as when the nuns were neighbours.
But the gift-shops stock their leprechauns
their báinín caps and sturdy black shillelaghs,
struggling to defeat
the long grey months of winter,
while every store will have its raffle
its Bingo or its Lotto to support
and the stress is on community,
on sport, or health, or farming;
and far too many sheep
graze on the hard-pressed grasslands
flattening the primroses, the violets and the bluebells,
and everywhere the ensuite guest-rooms
frilled with their window-boxes must be featured.
But the river sighs for stillness
and the rooks still call around Kilcolman's
and a poet labours near the lakeshore
and a painter runs a tiny gallery
opposite the bookie's.

A VILLANELLE

She still remembers but no longer cries
for he has banished all her foolish tears
her heart is heavy but her eyes are dry.

She turned to him for comfort but his eyes
were cold and reawakened lonely fears,
she still remembers but no longer cries.

The boating-party red on evening tide
led by Mountbatten then advanced in years
– her heart is aching but her eyes are dry.

His teenage grandson happy at his side
blotted out with others he held dear,
she will remember but no longer cries.

She walks along the lane at partner's side
knowing that tears will somehow wound his pride
her hands are shaking but her eyes are dry.

Some things she mourned have now been long put by
she cannot weep for them as once she did
she still remembers but her eyes are dry,
her heart feels arid but her head is high.

Vision

for Caroline Casey and the Ashling Project

Barebacked she sashays and sways
along her appointed way
lurching, swinging with her elephant-companion
to complete their celebrated journey,
adding a thread of Irish greenery
to the vast brown tapestry of India.

Smilingly Caroline has seen
how to unlock the coffers of the wealthy;
others now will look upon her world
and be the better for her
so-called blindness.

CHRISTMAS CANDLE

I wonder have we anything to say about your birth this
    Christmas?
We have so many other things to think of;
the parties and the crackers and the lights
will take priority
and then there's the stuffing for the bird
the wines and beer and spirits
the cards and holly
to be dealt with.

Oh what about that dainty jewelled cross
my daughter fancies?
maybe a cross is just a bit religious
but then it is so pretty.

I wonder have we anything to say about your birth this
    Christmas?
It's rather dreary thinking of a stable
when we should all be merry.
Of course we've heard about the angels and the shepherds
but they are hardly sexy?
It's just a story stemming from the past
while we have many modern things to handle.

Have you checked the programmes on TV
and be careful not to set the house on fire
with your Christmas candle!

Ferrycarrig

The cormorant raises wide angular wings
in salute to the winter sunshine,
the heron tucks in its jointed neck
as drifts of sandpipers swoop low and come to rest
beside it.
Herring-gulls and oyster-catchers
dance a black-and-white quadrille
with leisurely assurance
finding the grand new hotel
largely irrelevant.

Homeward the train beats through the copper countryside
to the lilt of bodhran, pipes and fiddle
the molten Slaney reflecting in black and tan
its fringe of biblical bulrushes;
passionate pink clouds flung across the sky
are telling of frost and ice to come.
At Bray the darkening sea is pinpointed
by the last of the Christmas lanterns.

Like the flocks of birds
man too can be courageous.

Connemara

It seems that everything that happens here is magnified
each leaf is twice as green, each spider matters more
than in the city. There is a sense of taking part in
ongoing drama or like voyaging
into unexplored territory.
You feel connected with your being in a deeper,
closer, way
and yet you know there are agendas
way beyond your own experience
happening all around you.

I understand now the old belief in fairies;
in this countryside you must make room
for questions greater than yourself.
in the city it is a matter of getting to
the supermarket or the dry-cleaners;
here those things may happen too but they are
    Separate.
always there is a
sense of otherness, of stronger influence,
of mystery.

The Sound of Silence

July deadline 1999

For all the weeks of tangled double-speak
for all the mound of media interviews
and confidential corridors
of conferences
the click of cameras
and the frantic snatch of sound bytes,
for all the talking up and talking down
of spin and counterspin
with dogged perseverance, enviable optimism,
there still remained
no letter in the post signed 'P. O'Neill'
and rows of empty leather seats in Stormont.

Bag-Lady

Where now
is the bleached linen and canvas lady
who used frequent the roads
and shore of my home town?
Dressed in loose sand-coloured clothes
and whitened tennis-shoes
she would move lightly, swiftly,
never looking anywhere
except to the beckoning sea,
not speaking to anyone
save sometimes to her God
in church.
Everything about her was sanded clean;
her shoulder-length silver hair gleamed
and the skin of her face and neck
was reddened by winds and sun and rains
and by her endless scrubbing.
What did she carry in her canvas bags?
A treasury of sea-shells I imagine;
what did she live on,
what did she eat?
Perhaps some milk or porridge
passed her lips
with maybe a treat of mushrooms
gathered at the dawn.
What happened to her,
where is she now?
God forbid that she is shut
in some confining place!
Better that she has walked bravely
into the accepting sea
and found a welcoming space
in which to rest
her bleaching bones.

Summer Storm

A great grey cloud envelops the mountains
to the west of Durrus
like a magician's cloak,
and soon the gutters of Cornamona
are splattering the Saturday streets
to freshen them for Sunday.
The lights are out in Oughterard,
leaving the houses floating
in amniotic twilight.
The television darkens
and guests in the B&B
are lit to bed with ornamental candles
from the smart new restaurant.
And I must do without my radio.
But faithfully
at five a.m. the dawn chorale
tunes up as usual.
This week it is the birds
and not the BBC
who will explain for me
their 'Something Understood'.

THE STRUGGLE

The molten lake is mauve, full of sweet reason,
each twig of the surrounding leafless trees
etched out against it
like delicate jet beading
against a satin bodice.
Today everything depicts serenity
or so it seems.
But, like myself, the lake is never certain
that tomorrow or even this afternoon
will not see a different story,
when ghosts and spectres of the past
and of the present too
descend on it to taunt it;
and all that seemed so simple and so calm,
so innocent and fail-safe,
is thrown into a cauldron of wild doubt,
evoking the apostles' terror
when, on another lake,
they cried out 'Save us, Lord, we perish!'

TABOOS

I have desired to go sometimes
where there are no taboos
where living would be clear, uncluttered,
no more confidences
behind closed doors
only nudists sitting bravely in their chairs
as in that photograph.
No secret places,
just everything exposed
and fully naked.
But I have known as well
that that is not the me
I most must live with,
the very private me
who needs her spaces
visibly defined,
who feels the pumice-stone of life
is rough enough
without the severing of screens,
the ripping of those veils
that give her shelter.
And life is life for me
just as it is for you
who brave the old taboos
and overturn them.
But my small Grandma smiled through tragic years
who, when I said I had miscarried,
gazed through the lace that veiled
her garden and replied
'It *is* a little cold, my dear,
for this the springtime of the year'.

THE GLANN ROAD

Just look for the sign at Oughterard
and go by Baurisheen, Foorannagh, Derrymoyle,
Gortdrishagh, Cappagarriff, Rinneroon
and winding on by Glann to Shannavock
follow the friendly road to the Hill of Doon.
In Spring it will sustain your spirit
with the miracle of crimson rhododendrons
or buds of soufflé pink and towering forest-flame
and the brassy cheerfulness of gorse,
the fidelity of primroses,
the genteel mauve of ladys smock
and a fringe of Mary's bluebells.
Beside a flowering orchard a scribe-in-residence
raises titian-haired children
and on the way the birds will sing
of life and love and of communion.
I know it sounds hyperbole unrhymed
but that's the way things are
in Spring on the Glann Road.

The Old Barracks at Glencree

The old lady clutches her shawl of clouds around her bony
shoulders
and gazes down the valley
hugging a dream that no one else can measure;
one day she will be filled again, she knows,
though clamorous rooks make nurseries in her hair
and the prying sky gapes in through rotting rafters.

'I will house peace' she says, 'a prince will come
from Wales to do me honour and I shall blend
the echoes of Welsh soldiers with sounds of children's
laughter
and the distinctive accents of the North'.

'Some will come here to pray' she says 'and some to build
and I shall reach them all because my bridge
will then be sturdy and I shall hold them in my house
in harmony'.

And so she dreams in solitude and silence,
confident of her appointed destiny.

- Glencree, February 2002

THE WRITER

In the service of words
I have clattered my keyboard
clicking my mouse
in search of that elusive phrase
that would adequately convey
my meaning.
But since what I want to tell
is life itself
no window will disclose
or capture it, leading it tamely
like a well-schooled pony
into my indoor manège.
The most that can be done
as Austen and Eliot knew
and Somerville and Ross continued
and Eavan Boland after
and many another
is just to lift a corner of a veil
permitting to come to view
a tiny cameo
that would otherwise have been
    unnoticed.

Discovery

Do not suppose your far-off sorrow buried
in leafy country graveyard
or under celtic cross and marble slab
in grey Glasnevin;
though honed and pumiced by long years of everyday
quite suddenly it still can ambush you
and grip your vitals,
as when a loving cousin lies
under the green and white and orange.

As long as you are you
it still survives.

THE OAK TREE

When I was young you were my rescuer,
my living Dunamase, my stronghold, guide and mentor;
a generous tree spreading its shade about me,
a friend always to be counted on
in time of trouble or anxiety.

The aged tree at last has fallen
leaving an aching hole behind it;
it just remains to pass its nourishment
to others coming after.

(For my cousin Tom O'Higgins)

SPRING 2003

Fog has been a feature of this springtime,
great hulking fog in which I try to find
a meaning for the torching of Baghdad
blazing on screens around the world the night before.
clouding, shrouding fog in which I search
for truth in the mouths of men in suits,
numbing freezing fog blotting out
the cherry trees and elegant magnolias
of suburban Dublin.
Few noises penetrate its blanket thickness
in the early mornings;
birds will take a lie-in till the sun at noon
will come to visit.
The only sound I now can hear is weeping
the sound of widows, parents, lovers
and the cries of children from their hospital beds
devoid of comfort.

After the Day of Mourning …

Yesterday we queued to sign the books
with our condolences,
to leave our flowers and our teddy-bears
as symbols of our loving;
yesterday we prayed in our cathedrals,
in chapels or in mosques,
in synagogues or in our private enclaves.
Yesterday we gazed at TV pictures
or listened to our radio
unwilling to switch off,
still grasping at those stories
and yet not fully comprehending.
Yesterday we felt a stir of national pride –
'How do you know a fireman?' someone asked;
'He's running the other way'
they gave the answer
'He rushes in while others stagger out – and many of
them Irish'.
But now today we must pick up
the fragments from the rubble
and somehow make enough reality
to go on living;
even the forlorn dogs
who only found those corpses
and the broken body parts
will have to pull themselves together
believing once again
that they are useful.

There yet remains a world out there
in need of service.

At Kenny's Bookshop

'A girl from the petshop up the road has died' it was announced
'and she will pass this way'.
The poets laid aside their festive wine
and stood in the darkened room
behind closed doors
facing the Galway rain.

Some thought of her traversing an endless plain
to nowhere,
some pictured God searching his vast pocket
for an ailing pup –
'Mind this one for me, Orla?'

Her friends walked sadly with her young remains,
if they hadn't weathered death before
they would again.

Crisis in the Church

Some of us seem not to have outgrown
the need to have our dolls all neatly dressed
and drinking tea together
out of their tiny tea-cups,
to wear our nurses' uniforms
with their bright red crosses,
or to unpack the bandages and stethoscopes
out of toy doctors' boxes.

But what to do now when the pain is real
and sharp and deep and adult
and writhing in the gut
is another matter;
no use trying to kiss it well
or to read from a fairy story.

The voice of the hare torn between hounds
cries shrill across our landscape
(as we have been reminded).

What songs have we to answer with,
to console and to assuage it?

How can we grow into a world
where the pain of victims
cannot be soothed by balm and sticking plaster?

First Communion

(a sequel to Denise Levertov's 'The Servant-Girl at Emmaus')

... so sure that when she brought the wine to table
it did not altogether come as a surprise
that he should smile and ask her just to wait
a moment. Then he dipped bread
into the wine and handed some to each
of his companions – AND TO HER!

'Eat this, do this' he said
'and please remember me'.

'Remember, Remember?'
sang her soaring heart
as she later washed the dishes
when the guests had all departed:

'As long as I'm alive
I shall remember him
and live in the memory
of this blessed day'.

SEEN FROM THE GAZEBO

The lake is wrinkled against the darkened shore
of a nearby island;
the sun glitters on closer, smoother waters
reminding of Christmas decorations
of silver foil and tinsel;
storm clouds have moved on southward
and the stately heron resumes his tranquil tour
with diplomatic gravity.

A pair of swans who've brought their children calling
for several generations
seem to have succumbed to the disease
of marital break-up.

He is now cavorting with a much younger female,
Still in her pinfeathers,
while his mate, not to be outdone,
has taken to a junior fellow-traveller.

What now of swans' monogamy,
– another fond belief exploded?

Hospitality

People go walkabout across my landscape,
many no longer living are yet alive to me
and still vibrate with zest
to the chords of my memory's heartstrings.
Inside my compound they are safe
from the threat of chill mortality;
they move in a coloured land
and speak in their own voices
where I am glad
to hear and share with them.

Friends still go walkabout across my landscape
whether they are dead or maybe
closed away in nursing-homes
not knowing truly who they are
or if they ever met me;
Nancy, Pat, May and Peggy –
oh, especially Peggy.

I laugh and chat with you the same as ever!
I call it hospitality, keeping a place for you,
not letting go, just holding on to you
as in the old days.

Just God

Details have always been a pain for me;
the names and years of wines, or species of plants,
or birds, or opus numbers of the music,
or recipes, or sporting teams
seldom remain –
only the fragrance, the taste, the flavour,
the marvellous 'birdness' of the creature,
the grace and courage of the players,
the sudden anguish of a cadence
or its mysterious assurance.

When someone speaks of God I like to hear,
God in the spare no-thingness of the deity, I mean,
not efforts to define, control, explain
and not the news of the foot-soldiers,
their holy networkings and tireless undertakings,
just God around, within, both them and me,
God in the quiet of a smile, a tear,
God in the freedom of abstractions,
in the silent grief of elephants over a dead companion
and in the buzzing of a sultry bee.

Questions

for HRH the Prince of Wales after his visit to Glencree,
15 February 2002

Why do I think you poor when you are rich,
rich beyond most men's imaginings?
But you seem poor, poor like a mendicant,
in robe of discipline, of service,
of tempered self-surrender.

Why when you have a lover do you
seem alone – you who one day will belong to everyone?
Is this what happens to a prince
who searches for the Spirit
hidden in the heart of everything?

On Hold

'Please hold' I am advised 'Please hold'
so I am holding
against a rising tide of doubt
I am still holding;
'Blessed are they who have not seen and yet believe' so I
keep holding,
though bulldozers have ruptured the mystique
that once knew poetry of psalms and lilt of litanies,
– 'rosa mystica, turris eburnea, stella matutina' –
and the quiet passion of stained-glass loveliness
no longer glows in convent sanctuaries,
only raw red-bricked alleyways named 'Convent Walk'
attempt to remind us now of what was ours.

And though I'm told
of indefensible happenings in the past,
of dark betrayals, gross depravities,
while it is customary to forget
the many kindnesses and self-sacrifices,
I still keep clinging to the beauty spread from You,
source of all our being,
poet, artist, craftsman, lover,
I am on hold!

AUTUMN IN GLANNROWAN

Blankly the neighbouring houses
stare back into our faces.
Children have taken from here
their surging joy and laughter on the water.
Now boats are hunched upon their sides,
like helpless invalids, and barbecues
no longer season evening breezes.
Fog in a great feather-duvet
suffocates the islands and
bushes are decked with jewelled frillies
spun by teams of spiders.
Silence is broken only
by the startled screech of a blackbird
sounding a frantic warning;
does she not know
that plans for spring are saved
in underground computers?

After Hillsborough

for Michael and Jane Lillis, November 1985

Oh let some laureate acclaim
not Reverend Paisley with his raucous cries
of 'Never, never, never!'
nor tight-lipped Molyneaux and angry crowds
wedged into grey Belfast
nor burning emblems fanned by orange glee
nor stalwart marchers led by fervent drums
with sashes of their fathers
– for they have had their full publicity –
but tell of those who, with a quiet mind,
knowing that rigid barriers must move,
dwell less on bitter rivalry than peace
and honour this Agreement

Remember too those colleagues from the South
shouldering their Northern tasks
with measured resolution. High though the price
steady their vocation. So will be raised
from a vague world of fond imaginings
a people bred in ancient aspiration
into the taut reality of here and now.
Through them this nation comes of age,
accepting its full responsibility.
Oh sing of all who with a cheerful heart
and unassuming laughter carry their load
with an amazing grace. May history
honour this new Agreement!

MEALS-ON-WHEELS
(in the inner-city 1970)

Dingy doorways, endless stairs,
musty odours! Household cares
unattended in my home,
extra rush this afternoon!
Wet today, an icy wind,
yet I'm glowing on my round –
with smiles and thanks and prayers untold
there's none support us like our old.

Indian Summer

Resurrection after the winter's ills
to sup with friends
from days you thought were over;
to wear, in your seventies,
red pointed shoes,
floating a chiffon scarf of many hues
and perfumed with Christmas luxury
behind you;
to be kissed by men
you've always been in awe of
who suddenly are saying you are lovely

With candlelight and wine
in this all-too-brief reunion
age and grey Monday mornings do not matter;
happiness is spread
by our birthday-host
and a long-time friend confides
that once he seriously
loved you!

The Passing of Paddy Matt

We thought of him as builder, boatman,
host of the neighbouring guesthouse;
it was only in his passing
we realised the measure of his story –
how from his early youth he had been a cornerstone,
an oaktree giving shade to many,
a constant in that lakeshore place
for more than eighty years,
a man for whom the preacher wept
lonely, remembering tears.

- Pentecost Octave 2001

RIA MOONEY

(founder of the Gaiety School of Acting)

She was a pint-sized lady
with fascinating face and voice
who could convey
the woes and wonders of the world
and its enthusiasms
with just a catch of breath
a twitch of eyebrow.
Her eyes could brim with sparkling joy
or deepest anguish all in a moment,
with hauteur she could even make herself seem tall
or with peasant plainness shrink inside
a low-set dwelling.

She was a Bessie Burgess, a Lady Bracknell,
a Rosie Redmond, Lyubov Andreyevna,
Romantic Countess Cathleen and, yes,
even an Uncle Vanya
but still to us she was Miss Mooney
who loved and understood her students
and, knowing which was feeling poorly,
could soothe a wretched stress filled headache
with hands-on kindness
lighting a rain-soaked winter evening
with her Dublin smile.

One Bread One Body

I've seen an ordained minister
shed tears of joy when he received
the Blessed Eucharist at a convent Mass
– but he was Presbyterian.
'Something I've wanted all my life to do'
– but he was Presbyterian.
In thirty years of sorrow I've heard voices
of faith and hope and love, courage
and sheer honesty
– but many are Presbyterian,
Methodist, Baptist, Anglican as well as
Roman Catholic and they are saying,
men and women, priests and sisters,
doctors, teachers, politicians,
– even our Head of State –
together saying
we need a place where we may celebrate
one Bread, one Body.

JUBILEE

for Eileen

Down polished corridors
I searched for Him
when I was a novice
hoping He might perhaps
smile from a painted canvas
or speak in the darkened Chapel
where glowing candles
and the prayers of sisters
produced a holy aura.

But He has kept faith in other ways
through other media;
in Scottish tones and Northern ones
and in those more familiar in the South
He has addressed me
sometimes in gentle, well-bred voices
but always in the rougher, harsher
accents of the poor.

THE LAST OF SUMMER

In shimmering unexpected heat
the swans have just called by
modestly showing off their teenage young
so proud of their survival.
All six cygnets still intact
have cheated hungry pike and prowling fox
thanks to parental watchfulness –
no mean achievement!
But the blue hydrangea bushes
– radiant, Wedgwood blue
like the 'Quink' on our schoolgirl pages –
are browning at the edges
and whispering an end to summer
in spite of the glowing sunshine;

Does a dying swan
truly save its only canticle of praise
for the day of desolation?

Family Gathering

The last car-door has slammed
and they have gone their separate ways
over the hillside.
It just remains
to tidy up the leavings,
remove the decorations,
saving gift wrappings for another day;
unwind the ribbons,
watch balloons deflate,
scatter the cake-crumbs for the blackbirds.
But hoard, hoard in the heart
all the precious moments
no camera can capture;
the sacrifices that were made to get here,
preparing of cards and gifts
the thought that went into that painting
of the beloved children,
and the courageous conquest of
what could have brought disaster.

Switch on the whirring laundry,
the freezer's already emptied
of the last of the packaged 'take-away's'.
Stock up instead with thankfulness
and the sustained belief
that in the end of all
even the one in sorrow
will somehow learn to be its master.

THE RURAL TIGER

I face four very doubtful cattle-grids
bent by the weight of trucks of nearby builders
and take the upper road, known as the scenic route,
(though the lower one is likewise beautiful)
I pick my way among the puddled potholes
which make a mockery of last year's improvements;
and I pray I will not meet the foresters'
double-articulated lorry nor the garbage truck
nor any other great 'long vehicle'
and that the low-slung winter sun won't blind my eyes
as I negotiate that awkward bend,
and that the collie dog won't mount an angry protest
as I pass the Fairy Bridge, nor fatuous cattle
stand munching in the roadway,
nor small boy seek his errant ball
out from between the bushes
as I approach the Senior School, hoping the students,
will have parked their L-plate cars or motor-bikes
before I get there.
I wiggle across the uphill twisted bridge weaving between
Bus Eireann and the giant JCB's
engaged in knocking down the convent
– (thus making room for twelve new 'luxury'
    apartments) –
and the panting Euro-lorries
pounding their way to Connemara.

At last I reach the newsagent and gather up my paper –
'Isn't the Dublin traffic terrible?' they say 'You're so much
safer in the country'.

A Northern Miscellany

I travelled when I was seven
to take part in the Belfast Feis
thinking that it was heaven
to have a new blue velvet dress
with its sash of beautiful satin
and a cloud of white lace at my neck.

But the dour forbidding houses
bordering the railway track
and the grey smoke-belching chimneys
darkening the sea of the Lough ...
and did some of those other children
grow up to buy fish at Frizelle's,
dine out at La Mon, pray at Darkley
(where no word of anger was said)?

And for marvellous summers after
we frolicked at far Inishowen
battling the wild surging breakers,
collecting the near-precious stones,
invading the neighbouring kitchens
for buttery, luscious drop-scones
or gorging huge teas at the convent
in nearby Derry (never Londonderry).

But the fluttering July bunting
observed from the train on the way
and the Union Jacks crowning church
steeples
there'd have to be trouble some day;

and did children who screamed then in
    laughter
grow later to cry out in pain?
A sense of impending disaster
was beginning to form in my brain.

Yes the long tortured years lay before us
when Derry was showered with shame,
Belfast coloured red on a Friday
when, at fifteen, young Stephen was slain
because he was helping his neighbours
– and his killing was done in my name ...

And oh the doughty ladies
wrapped in their Union flags
and the lonely hunger-strikers
huddled in filthy rags
and the bodies, and portions of bodies
packed into plastic bags.
And the pinched old-young faces of
    children
buying gifts at the Christmas bazaars
and the worn old-young faces of parents
and the sleek well-groomed silvery hair
of the Secretary of State at the Service,
and surgeons trying to stitch together
what man had blown asunder.

And the tiny white-washed backyards
and the spotless front-door steps
and the cherished family albums
so memories be kept
and the splendid, powerful roadways
– but the haemorrhaging of the best.

And the drooping, draylon dressing-
gowns
and rollers in the hair
and the stacks of tranquillisers
that just might help you bear
the stare of the backward-pacing,
gun-at-the ready squaddies
who wish that they were not there.

But the fresh winding road to Corrymeela
and at times in the thrill of that bay
memories of pure blue velvet
– and Kintyre on a very clear day
and the healing of some from dark 'romper-rooms'
and laughter from prisoners' young
and instead of the thump of the lambeg
a bell calls that
God's praises be sung.

January Blues

Before the dawn I had a knowledge of my Maker
I sensed that in the quiet dark of fossil-water
the Spirit lies, and in the fleeting fragrance
of sweet blossoms the scented goodness of the Godhead
can be savoured. I heard the ripples of God's music
in the underlying chords of my existence,
I touched the silken strength of God's own skin
in fruits and flowers,
I laughed at the Creator's humour in fancy fishes,
admired the feathered patterns and designs
of the sophisticated sculptor;
I wondered at the marvels of the rainbow,
replied 'Amen' to blackbird's sleepy singing.
I danced and swayed to rhythms deep within me
accepting they were there for my delighting.
I played at hide-and-seek among the bushes
of my fancies, knowing all the time it was the Spirit
was my playmate. A grandchild's gurgling laughter
echoed strains
of God's own singing
and nothing mattered since the world was cherished.

But came the dawn and then the challenge
to bring this loving Lord
into the here and now of lukewarm living;
the wind is sharp, the news is bleak, the churchbells
unappealing
and, mounted once again upon its treadmill,
my January mind insists
on picking out the foibles of my friends
and not their healing.

The Fright of our Lives

Supposing that you were not there for me
if I should turn around
and you were not in sight?
Surely then I would forget the ways
in which I feel you undervalue me
and grow to realise
that in my partnered need of you
nobody else will do?
Though others paint a certain dream for me
blotting you for a time out of my sight
they do not know the inner core of me
the way you do;
they have not made the journey
we two "only children" made together.
They'd have a lot of catching up to do
if I should look around and not see you;
then, in my fright, I'd call for you
and you would answer,
    wouldn't you?

Daisy Days

Striding on safari to the markets
or garden-centres of suburban Ireland
blow-dried Mná na hÉireann, in designer jeans
and so-called casual jackets,
target their quarry, urging their children on
to sit astride that tiger;
but all the time depressions deepen
and the lonely find few ears to listen,
save maybe the hundred thousand strangers
who tune in to the radio
while immigrants are searching
for one hundred thousand more
                                    to bid them welcome.

Did the prophet fear those contradictory tones
staining the State's foundation,
bright green spilling on darker stones
and traces of black and tan
still left on the new-born nation?
Could a path be steered through the white of peace
to link with the loyal orange,
would purple mountains glowing bright
in the golden hope of Collins
be disfigured soon by a crimson tide
of fratricidal carnage?

(Oh best man, friend o' mine Rory,
you will not now survive
to sponsor the infant's glory).

Peace Process

on the eve of President Clinton's visit
December 1995

'They haven't gone away, you know'
those hooded warriors armed with their baseball bats,
their bombs, their unrelenting Semtex
and their obsessional minds
convinced of their own rectitude,
believing they are the sole keepers
of the sacred flame of Irishness,
fed upon one-eyed history,
blind to the plight of others,
deaf to those doctrines that are not their own,
silently dealing retribution
in line with their austere code
of bloodstained brotherhood.
They haven't gone away, you know,
but we must trust the one who tells them now
that violence is of the past
and we must grasp that Sinn Fein hand,
daring to tread the narrow swaying bridge,
leading, we hope, towards peace.

EXPLORATION

As long as there are ladies left
with pearls and bouffant hair-do's
and bridge-parties and bracelets
and flesh-coloured silk stockings
then we maintain
some linkage with a past that seemed to hold
security for our mothers;
but what shall we do without them
when they're gone,
we in our anoraks and jeans,
our track-suits and our trainers?
Can we be sure
we know where we are going
as we scan the stars
surveying the new campaigns
to leave this world in spaceships
reaching out, perhaps,
to Mars?

End of the Writer's Workshop

How can they turn and leave
as if they'd never shared their secrets
with me – awakening my own beginnings?
Recounted their childhood pleasures
and the collegiality of student coffees,
whispered their sorrows – how it felt
to slip from mother's knee and not recovered,
painted with vibrant colours the fall in Canada,
captured the shrill delight of dogs on morning scampers,
sketched torrid days on Moorish beaches,
breathed the hot breath of Spanish lovers
or embraced by the River Lee?
Have brought me hatted and gloved to the Park Races,
have entered delivery-wards and emerged with baby
    bundles,
reminded how it feels to be outnumbered
by adolescent boyish energies,
told of the dedication and stupidity of former teachers,
moaned about their bunions or the drone
of Granma's snoring,
remembered Demeen on a Dingle beach
or bumped into an erstwhile sweetheart
on the street in Cobh,
stirring my being as when
those childhood globes of glass were shaken
and snow swirled round inside them
or when gazing in a kaleidoscope
I marvelled at its myriad patterns.

But now they must turn and wave Goodbye
leaving only their generosity
to be remembered and treasured,
remembered and treasured.

Radio God

It must be lonely to be broadcasting your love –
do many listen?
And if they stumble on your station
do they drown your messages
with anthems and with songs
of their own making?
Turn up the sound a bit
and sharpen up your signal;
some of us are getting hard of hearing
and so much else is claiming our attention
while all around is background noise
or atmospheric interference.
I know that you prefer to speak in silence
Spirit to spirit
but in this Jubilee Year
could you not please, just for this once,
increase your volume?

RADIO FOUR – LONG WAVE

BBC World Service (through the night)

I dreamt it was a dream
that forty men were massacred
close to their home in Kossovo

and it was a dream
about President Clinton's impeachment
who never even heard of Monica Lewinsky
– only the poems of Maya Angelou.

I dreamt the British diplomat had said
she felt certain of the Good Friday Agreement;
I pondered on the musings of Marcus Aurelius
and wondered if, in the end of all,
life itself is just a dream
without a meaning?

Advice to a Growing Girl

If you have the courage of Bernadette Devlin,
then steadfastly say what you know is true
and do what you must do
according to your conscience;
so you will live at peace with your own mind,
though never finding ease
in your uncompromising life.

But I have settled for half-truths and smiled
and sat at laden tables
and lulled malaise about inequalities
by thinking 'What's the use?
What can one woman do
in seas of platitudinous hypocrisy?'

Yet now I know!
Yes, I have seen brave women in my day,
read Dervla Murphy's pioneering escapades,
watched Kennedy wives support those shattered heads
and not give way.
(So in an earlier day it was accomplished in my own
home).

But maybe one time too
these women were uncertain girls like you
who had to teach themselves to rise?
Oh maybe one day, Iseult, you'll surprise us so
and be the leaven in the midst
of our complacent dough!

- *'White Lodge' 1975*

TWENTIETH CENTURY REVISITED

It isn't comfortable to be revisionist
stare into the eyes of a lost leader
while questioning his values,
take down the busts of heroes from their columns
and lose them in the attics of the memory,
remove their pictures from the walkways of the mind,
pass by their monuments. But it may be
that they were premature in their ambitions;
and when the blood was young and hot, with pulses
    racing,
they undertook a war of separation
which might have been avoided.

Maybe this blood-stained century
now should be granted leave of absence
or amnestied in mothballs,
and the indomitable Irishry of North and South
should gaze into the faces of their children
and not their ancestors
while planning for the future.

- Glannrowan 1999

From Lithuania with Love

She stood tall and straight like a silver taper
sharing her incandescent joy with those around her.
Like an Amnesty candle shining through the wire
she spoke of a foreign place and other people
where now in sisterhood of prayer
she finds her future.

ADVENT PRAYER

The little ones pedal and scoot their way
braving the uphill puddled path
to their creches and kindergartens,
accompanied by mothers pushing buggies
and by their enthusiastic dogs.
A blackbird fidgets urgently in the copper hedge
as orange cotoneaster replaces languid lavender.
Sharpen our focus now to comprehend your coming
with all the zest and confidence of childhood
into your difficult, dangerous and largely
    inattentive
    World.

The Angel

At first I didn't know she was an angel,
the bobbly lady in another lane
in rush-hour morning traffic,
all golden curls and rings and many bracelets
and ornaments and pretty painted fingers.

'What can I do to help?' she called
but I was too distressed to focus;
with engine running I'd not exactly stalled
at the five-road intersection
but all the same the car just would not budge
while anger mounted in the barping rows behind me.

'I'll run for help' I cried
'back to the garage up the road
where it has just been serviced'.
'And I'll wait here' she reassured
'to mind your keys and your belongings'.
When I returned on wobbly legs
with the concerned mechanic
there was my unoffending car all neatly parked
beyond the lights beside the path
and giving no-one bother.

'Angel' I said (by then I had a glimmer of her provenance)
'just how on earth did you persuade it?'
Smiling she handed back the keys
and melted into the teeming, throbbing traffic
I blew my thank-you kisses to the skies
in the direction of her homeland
for earth was not her bailiwick.

Feast of All Saints

The lake was silver and still
save for the hermit heron
silent among the rushes
down by Paddy's harbour;
boats lay propped upon their floorboards,
out in the bay a few mergansers
sported on All Saints Day
while from behind the pleated hills
the radiant saints sent down their mother-of-pearl
    assurance
in shining white and blue;
'It's true, it's true!'
Binmen, professors, children, charwomen
faxed in the sky
the joyful news of their glad feasting
and the waters too
reflected it between the leafless branches;
'Good news, good news! We're all en fête' they said,
'How could you ever doubt it?'

An Easter Hymn

'Oh let her be,
for she has done a lovely thing for me'
he said, when generously she brought the alabaster jar
for his anointing. And so his loneliness was eased
and her extravagance became economy.
Veronica offering a tender towel,
needing to show her deep solicitude,
Simon lending a shoulder strong when his was weak,
the blind, believing thief in shared disgrace,
whenever there is sung the Easter hymn
we celebrate them, thankful there were some
who, in their characteristic ways,
could sweeten even such an agony.

The Mulberry Bush

The women prisoners
repeating their simple song
circle their only tree
in every weather

endorsing their sisterhood
establishing their own identity
taking a certain charge
of their situation

raising their voices high
over granite walls
to fashion a nursery rhyme
for their children's children

hoping a miracle might grow
out of the humble worms
who in time might learn to spin
from sow's ears some silken purses.

A Housewife's Te Deum

More lightsome that egg-whites all fluffy with air,
more bright than the sheen on my small daughter's hair,
more sure than a surgeon's skilled, competent care –
your happiness fills me, O God.

More clear than the sky in the first morning light,
more shining than furniture polished and bright,
more warm than the turf-glow that comforts at night –
your happiness fills me, O God.

More loving than mothers when little ones pray,
more fragrant than blossoms on delicate spray,
more splendid than music fine orchestras play –
your happiness fills me, O God.

More tranquil than rainbows after the rain,
more gentle than kisses that soothe away pain,
more vibrant than colour, more flashing than flame –
great happiness thrills me, my God!

- 'White Lodge' 1968

IF I SHOULD SING …

If I should sing of you, Thérèse, I'd tell
not of the fair-haired child whom once I loved,
petted by older sisters and a widowed Dad,
rubbing the soapsuds in her eyes for love of Jesus,
seeing her letter 'T' traced in the stars,
winning her way to Carmel from a startled Pope.

Fifteen, they said, was much too young,
though probably Mary was not more
when she pronounced her 'fiat'
and certainly Anne Frank by then
was woman enough to understand herself
before she died in Belsen.

But, if I'd write of you, Thérèse, I'd celebrate
the near-débâcle of your passing,
the agony of doubt, the hovering on the edge of
faithlessness,
the 'little flower' by then so pierced with thorns
like those around the head of Him
who thought He was forsaken.

Oh, I would sing of this, Thérèse, so that the world would
know
that saints can be severely tempted,
and yet, like Peter, be recovered.
I would forget the statues and the showers of roses
and I would say 'This woman feared
and with her Lord descended into hell
before she knew the blessed light of heaven'.

Sunday in Mayfly Time

No time to dither now – the fly has risen!
Old men forgetting aches and pains
leave it to boys to bargain by the roadside
over drowsy flies asleep in fathers' boxes
and head across the water,
the light of heaven in their faces.

There has to be forgiveness the preacher said this
    morning
or else there is no loving in our orbit
and so all must live forgivingly, woman and man too.
Forgiving nature when it thwarts and disappoints us,
forgiving animals and neighbours
and the maelstrom of confusion
that may attend our being.

But now the therapeutic fly has risen
and far across the lake a fish is leaping,
while the drone of outboard engines excites the gentle
    breezes
and occasionally a cuckoo sings from the wooded islands
and a sense of 'now' is vibrantly astringent,
of being on the edge of some discovery
because the fly has risen!

LÁ 'LE BHRIGHDE
1 FEBRUARY 2002

We thought it was the first of Spring
but maybe Mary of the Gael
is raining down displeasure
because the day is one of fearful storms
and flooding. Firemen and police
are rescuing old people from their houses,
boats and canoes are rowed along city streets,
a frightened cat is perched on her owner's shoulders
as he struggles, laden with belongings,
through murky water
just around the corner
in nearby Irishtown.

TODAY
1 FEBRUARY 2002

In this pearl-grey in-between time
I try to write before
the duties of the day
take over from
the cobwebs of my dreams
and it becomes more urgent
to go out and shop
than to live within the private
wider world I sense at night.

But the cobwebs disappear
even as I touch them,
blown by the winter gales
or by the summer's vibrant bird-song.
Where now those finer thoughts
that seemed to need recording?

The reality that is me is once more active
and today will not be one for creativity.

RESURRECTION
(EASTER 1998)

'Will someone roll away the stone for us?' they wondered.
Out of the darkness of despairing grief
they still remembered practicalities
– as women mostly do –
and funeral rites awaited full completion,
balm must be poured anew.

But who would move those other stones, they pondered;
the leaden heartsore weights within their breasts,
how would they deal with their own shattered longings,
the hopes destroyed, the sickening pain;
would spring for them be ever rediscovered,
would love return again?

Can angels in Ireland roll back what divides us,
roadblocks of fratricide, barriers of hate
boulders of bitterness, gulfs of depression,
loneliness, drug-abuse, how shift such weight?
But Love can renew us at this time of Rising
demolishing fear-studded fences of spite,
dismantling with laughter the sway of the cynic.
At Easter we count on new love and new life.

Peace

Behind locked doors they shared their anguished
thoughts
about the crucifixion of their leader
spiked with a complexity of fear, of anger and self-
loathing
since only one had not abandoned him.
That upper room spoke its reproaches to them
of broken bread dipped in the wine with him,
of splashing soothing water with the cool care of towels

as he had washed and dried their dusty faltering feet
a few days earlier. What lay ahead?
To follow him they had forsaken everything;
what now remained of former lives
to carry on with?
Mary of Magdala was convinced
that she had spoken with him in the graveyard
another two believed that he had talked with them
while walking to Emmaus.
Supposing it were true what was he thinking
of their own betrayal?

When suddenly he stood there in the midst of them,
smiling, easy, natural, blessing them with peace
and teasing those who thought he was a ghost
by sitting down and eating fish with them
as in the old days. The room again was radiant with joy
while the peace which he had breathed on them
poured oil on smarting wounds, on sickening doubts,
never again to leave them.

From Pardon and From Protest

I am from heads held high, stiff upper lips
and "the Clan's" affectionate laughter
where the pain was seldom spoken to the children
– and never among the teacups.

I am from Celtic spirals and the unresolved riddles
of twisted serpents scrolled on holy pages;
I am from dancing-class and make-believe
and graven plaque on cenotaph unheeded.

I am from motherhood and meetings
and an unrelenting trail of grocery trolleys;
I am from history and politics
and letters to the press and pictures of my father.

I am from lines of pilgrims thumbing beads upon their
    journeys,
from surgeon's spattered vests and the near-certainty of
    an all-loving Godhead
I am from pardon and from protest – and like the spirals
I return to where I came from.

For the Freedom Fighters

How is it possible to deal out death
while spiders weave their jewelled miracles
through mists of morning heather
wrapping the moors in filigree adornment,
while song-birds fling their 'Alleluias' to the skies
and butterflies besiege the buddleias
in confident renewal?

How is it possible to plan for death
while small boats tumble on a buoyant lake
and cuckoos call from rural fastnesses
where honeysuckles clamber through the hedgerows?
How plan to kill where blackberries
redden the searching fingers with sweet juices,
not blood sacrifice?

How execute life's end while faithfully
dark winters germinate their secret plans
preparing resurrection? How share
in spring's glad seminars while choking out
the life-breath of another – claiming
that this will foster union?
Name your campaign
as hatred or revenge, but leave aside
your fallacy of fusion!

AFTER DRUMCREE 1998

What does it matter by which road you walk
to Portadown? You still are you
and nothing in the pavements of Garvaghy
will make you different. The air
is no more healthy there
and you are no more free
because you march in front of Catholics,
wearing your sashes, banging your drums
to honour your tradition
and conserve your culture.

Say, is it likely those who perished at the Somme
would understand the deaths of three young children
as hallowing their memory?
What does it matter now how you return
to your home-town?

A Rite of Passage

Yes, Santa's brought the bike you've dreamed of,
purple, proud, magnificent,
just like the one you friend has,

and you're wearing your 'cool' black trouser-suit
with glossy patent boots and dangly ear-rings
and your nails are tinted almost to match your cycle
while your starry eyes are shining.

But try as he might
Santa has failed to find
that which you most have need of
and though they smile, politely pulling crackers,
two families are grieving.

Forgiveness

So there he stood upon the shore
with everything in waiting.
The fire was going well,
fresh fish were grilling
and they would bring some more
(this would confirm their own importance).
And at that Easter breakfast
he would hear from Peter
just how much he loved him
No decommissioning of the past
nor rank betrayals would be mentioned
simply 'Bring more fish' and 'Do you love me?'

Today as mists clear from the Agreement,
hammered in Belfast last Good Friday evening,
a voice speaks from far South Africa
of truth and reconciliation
and puts a definition on forgiveness;
'It is', the bishop says,
'a way of dealing with the past
so as to plan the future'.
Poor Peter's past had been disastrous
but he was asked to bring along his gifts
of fish and loving;
nothing more was needed
to complete this paschal sharing
and look towards the future.

EPIPHANY

Against an opalescent sky of palest pink
the church spire beckons
through dark mesh of black and leafless trees
and chorus of encircling crows
announcing today's strange story;
how wise men travelled from afar
bearing their seeming inappropriate gifts
and following that brilliant star
found you – not in any regal state –
but wrapped in God's compassionate glory

NEW YEAR'S EVE 2000

The wise men found you by a single star
but we with our advanced technology
must replicate its brightness
by multi-coloured millions
searing the darkened heavens
with the brilliance of our messages,
looping the sparkling necklace of our lights
around the united globe
so all can recognize its meaning.

What meaning?
Is it thank-you
that you cared enough to come
and live among us?
Is it a sign of one meeting another
at your party
and lighting hosts of candles to dispel
the darkness of the needy?
Now that we have had our celebrations,
erected monuments, lit up our proudest buildings
with the clamour of fireworks and of carillons of bells
in our remembering eardrums,
can we but hold the memory
of a rejoicing world
and come to understand again
why we are happy?

Nob Hill
San Francisco

The cheerful boats bob calmly in the Bay
while screeching jets tear their aerobic path
across the cobalt sky. Bowed Oriental gran'mas
fill plastic bags with other people's rejects;
(perhaps they, too, look forward to recycling?)
In Grace Cathedral Francis is remembered
with frescoes, carvings and a Christmas crib
though parks are closed at night against the homeless;
With dawn emerge the joggers and the keep-fits
while Chinatown retains the morning-rites
of a more ancient day
and O.J. found 'Not Guilty' continues to hold the nation
in his unblinking sway.

CHILDHOOD IN THE PALE

Apart from the blessed saints
the people most affecting me in youth
were Shirley Temple, Deanna Durbin,
Judy Garland and the small princesses
Elizabeth and Margaret Rose,
beautiful in party-dresses,
Snow White and the Seven Dwarves,
Jeanette McDonald with her Nelson Eddy,
the Scarlet Pimpernel and dancing Pomona
with Pauline and their little sister Posy
And the girls of the Chalet School.

All of my stories had their happy endings;
you would come blinking to the street
knowing that good would always triumph
or when you put the book down you'd be sure
your friends would live in happiness for ever.
(The only one I ever met was stately Shirley Temple
in low-cut gown and very serious with jet-black hair,
by then US Ambassador to the United Nations).

All of my stories had their happy endings
no matter what the problem;
none of it touched on the truth that I had come from,
that left me fatherless;
that, as the saying goes, was altogether other.

WARRIORS

for the Carmelite Sisters in Kilmacud

'The sisters are engaged in prayer', the message said
'and they will phone you later';
engaged in prayer –
a dozen women glorifying God,
a dozen midwives cradling a suffering world
and handing it tenderly to its Creator,
a dozen sisters living frugally
but spendthrifts in love for one another
twelve people pleading with their maker,
twelve faithful voices singing praises,
who'll fight for you against your enemy
of darkness or despair
and fling themselves against the sufferings
of your neighbours.

MEMORY

There is an azalea with a certain flower
of shocking orange sherbet
which with its special fragrance
can suddenly transport me to a hillside bower
of near-forgotten girlhood's hopes and dreams
its unrealities – and its devastating loneliness.

WONDERS

Yes, it is true
the less well-off
know more about reality
than others do
whom money shelters
but all the same
I've seen amazing things
my forebears never dreamed of.

I've seen a pope
go pilgriming to Canterbury
and I've felt the scald of sudden tears
when cardinal red
first coloured
Belfast's long grey Anglican Cathedral.
I've proudly watched
two mothers of young children
inspect a Presidential guard-of-honour
at what was first
the residence of the Viceroy
and I've heard a wailing didjeridu
call back across the endless years of dreaming
and of mysterious inheritance
binding the then with what we know as now,
focusing thought on You
whom I've been privileged to share
as Eucharistic minister.

Sunday in Ordinary Time

The fog is thick this morning,
not fragile, lacy, delicate
but heavy, damp and uninviting,
shrouding the scarlet creepers,
cotoneasters and the carmine apples.
The feathered bamboo sprays
are bowed with moisture,
though struggling to retain some dignity,
like tipsy ladies coming from a levee.

The morning news is grim
more murders, bombings and duplicity
and yet a single robin dares to sing
of hope and unadulterated innocence.

Reconciliation Rainbow

Out of the sum of our believings,
out of our painful disagreements,
out of our doubtings and withdrawings
out of the slogging and the hauling,
out of the mud and isolation
out of the pain of separation,

somehow, some way, we idealistic people
each placed our special piece in the mosaic
building a bridge of hope and peace
Together
our reconciliation rainbow.

- for James and Sarah, Pat and (the late) Lil, for Ivo, for Frank, for Mai and Rachel and Judy and the very many others who suffered deeply because of their commitment to Glencree

from Una with love -

December Dawns

Just when all thoughts of courage seem quite moribund
and mediocrity may rule O.K.
and you can safely munch your chocolates
settling for soft complacency
– 'Because I'm worth it' –

Just when you think that you have reached the age
when disciplines may be forgotten
and nothing's worth much effort any more
since you are now retired
– and almost past it –

Then you are confronted by stark crimson dawns,
vibrant, electric, challenging,
across dark dormant waters
and then you know that there is no escape
but to respond to light with answ'ring torch
– and to keep with it –

UNA O'HIGGINS O'MALLEY: AN APPRECIATION

Conor Brady

On a sunny Spring morning in 1973 I drove out from Dublin through the Phoenix Park to 'White Lodge' to meet Una O'Higgins O'Malley for the first time.

I was researching a postgraduate thesis, focusing on the period 1922–32 and the setting up of the Irish police (the Garda Siochana) the courts and the administration of justice. The energised, driving figure of Kevin O'Higgins – Una's father – appeared everywhere in the sources I was using. I felt I wanted to know more about the man, to get the sense of his personality. So I wrote to her. And she invited me to visit and to talk.

Many of the people who participated in the independence struggle were still alive at this time and I had interviewed some, as well as members of their immediate families. It had been, on the whole, a somewhat depressing experience for a young graduate student. I had encountered many entrenched positions and much residual anger. I found only a few instances of striking broadmindedness or forgiveness. There was little sense of generosity across the divide of the Civil War. And once or twice, I found, it was the offspring of the former-combatants, rather than the veterans themselves, who were the more entrenched.

That morning encounter at 'White Lodge' left me with an enduring sense of having, at last, met someone who was not imprisoned by past wrongs, real or imagined.

Una was not the only exception in my sequence of depressing interviews. But she was by far the most forthcoming and outspoken. Even then, it was clear, she had worked through the issues of loss, of separation, of forgiveness, of reconciliation. She sat in her home that morning and spoke quietly but certainly of what her father had hoped to achieve for Ireland, of the loss which his assassination brought to her and to her family, of the role which he had played as the 'hard man' of the Provisional Government, as it set about putting down its enemies with a programme of execution and imprisonment.

Quietly but cogently she set out the reasons, as she saw them, why he did what he had to do. Then she set out the reasons why those who took the other side did what they felt they had to do. At that time, there was little known about the identities of the men who killed her father in July 1927. But even then she could speculate calmly on their motivation, even as she expressed her revulsion – and her forgiveness – for what they did.

In truth, as I recall it, she had little enough to tell me of substance in regard to my thesis. I was enriched however in understanding. I came away with a sense of admiration and respect that has endured down all the years I have known her since. As I have watched her and listened to her various forays into the forum of ideas and public dialogue, I have often thought how proud her dying father would have been had he been able to see or to listen forward through the decades, as his younger daughter proclaimed her values across Irish public life.

Her contribution to the life of modern Ireland has been singular. She has been a constant witness for tolerance, for forgiveness, for reconciliation.

In the 16 years during which I was editor of *The Irish Times* (and for a good few years before that while I was a senior editor), Una's activities would appear with regularity on the daily news schedules: she was running a conference at Glencree, putting a picket on the Sinn Fein office, organising a petition to some government department, setting up a lecture by some figure of reconciliation from the international scene. Occasionally, there would be a telephone call or a note asking for coverage. The newspaper's exertions were invariably rewarded with good copy from a seminar, a march or a meeting.

Then the Books Editor, Caroline Walsh, came in to me one day with a copy of Una's first book, *From Pardon and Protest: memoirs from the margins.* I read it over the coming days – and as I did so came to understood that I had only seen one dimension of this remarkable person.

As I went through *From Pardon and Protest* I realised that it was inviting me to look into the inner psyche of a still-sorrowing child, parted from a loving father while still in babyhood. I was invited to trace the difficult years of a sensitive young girl, watching her widowed mother try to re-order her own life while preparing her daughters for the world. I was following a problematic but tender narrative of a progression from girlhood into adulthood, into marriage, motherhood and middle-age. I am not an overly-literary person, but in Una's prose – and especially in her poetry – I found a universality of human experience that moved me more than I could ever have expected.

Perhaps I found some resonances with my own life experience – for my father died when I was quite young. Her poem *A Widow's Child* expressed perfectly for me the mixture of bewilderment, concern, sorrow, anger (and, in time, comprehension) with which a child may view a surviving parent when the other has died.

Elsewhere, the poetry has echoes of Eavan Boland:

I am from motherhood and meetings
And an unrelenting trail of grocery trolleys
I am from history and politics
And letters to the press and pictures of my father.

Much of Una's poetry is deeply personal, anchored in the fundamental things of the human condition, birth, death and the progress of children through the passages of life. Much of it reflects Una's religious commitment and its interaction with her political activism.

Her language is simple but wonderfully crafted. Unadorned, everyday language is wrought into statements and messages that are complete – and probably beyond improvement. In the title-poem of this collection, *Twentieth Century Revisited,* she writes this:

Maybe this blood-stained century
Should now be granted leave-of-absence
Or amnestied in mothballs
And the indomitable Irishry of North and South
Should gaze into the faces of their children
And not their ancestors
While planning for the future.

If only, I thought, when I read that, I could have written editorials that said it all so well!

Read *Twentieth Century Revisited* and her memoirs *From Pardon and Protest* to deepen one's understanding of the story of Ireland, good and bad, during the 20th century. But read them also as a story, beautifully and sensitively written, of an Irish woman's journey through a life at once very ordinary and very exceptional.

Dublin, 10 April 2003